W9-BGU-505

DATE DUE

This Is What I Want to Be

Police Officer

Heather Miller

Heinemann Library
Chicago, Illinois

©2003 Reed Educational & Professional Publishing
Published by Heinemann Library,
an imprint of Reed Educational & Professional Publishing
Chicago, IL

Customer Service 888-454-2279
Visit our website at www.heinemannlibrary.com

Designed by Sue Emerson, Heinemann Library
Printed and bound in the United States by Lake Book Manufacturing, Inc.

07 06 05 04 03
10 9 8 7 6 5 4 3 2 1

Library of Congress Cataloging-in-Publication Data
Miller, Heather.
    Police officer / Heather Miller.
        p. cm. — (This is what I want to be)
Includes index.
Summary: A simple introduction to the equipment, uniform, daily duties, and other aspects of the job of a police officer.
    ISBN: 1-4034-0371-6 (HC), 1-4034-0593-X (Pbk.)
    1. Police—Juvenile literature. 2. Law enforcement—Vocational guidance—Juvenile literature. [1. Police. 2. Occupations.] I. Title.
    HV7922.M48 2002
    363.2'023'73—dc21

                    2001008138

Acknowledgments
The author and publishers are grateful to the following for permission to reproduce copyright material:
p. 4 Scott Barrow/International Stock; p. 5 EyeWire Collection; pp. 6, 11 Mark C. Ide; pp. 7L, 20 Bob Daemmrich/Stock Boston; p. 7R Elena Rooraid/PhotoEdit; p. 8 Corbis Stock Market; p. 9 Richard Hutchings/Photo Researchers, Inc.; p. 10L Roy Morsch/Corbis Stock Market; p. 10R DiMaggio/Kalish/Corbis Stock Market; pp. 12, 13 Scott Braut; p. 14 Table Mesa Productions/Index Stock Imagery, Inc.; p. 15 A. Ramey/PhotoEdit; p. 16 Michael Heller/911 Pictures; p. 17 Chuck Szymanski/International Stock; p. 18L David R. Frazier/Photo Researchers, Inc.; p. 18R Mark E. Gibson/Mira.com; p. 19L Scott Alfieri/Getty Images; p. 19R Phil Martin/Heinemann Library; p. 21 Linda Phillips/Photo Researchers, Inc.; p. 23a (row 1, L-R) David Woods/Corbis Stock Market., Richard Hutchings/Photo Researchers, Inc., Mark E. Gibson/Mira.com; p. 23 (row 2, L-R) Don Farrall/PhotoDisc, Mark C. Ide, Chuck Szymanski/International Stock; p. 23 (row 3, L-R) Mark C. Ide, A. Ramey/PhotoEdit, Roy Morsch/Corbis Stock Market; p. 23 (row 4, L-R) DiMaggio/Kalish/Corbis Stock Market, Corbis Stock Market, Corbis Stock Market

Cover photograph by Bill Fritsch/Brand X Pictures
Photo research by Scott Braut

Special thanks to our advisory panel for their help in the preparation of this book:

Eileen Day, Preschool Teacher
Chicago, IL

Ellen Dolmetsch, MLS
Wilmington, DE

Kathleen Gilbert,
Second Grade Teacher
Austin, TX

Sandra Gilbert,
Library Media Specialist
Houston, TX

Angela Leeper,
Educational Consultant
North Carolina Department
of Public Instruction
Raleigh, NC

Pam McDonald, Reading Teacher
Winter Springs, FL

Melinda Murphy,
Library Media Specialist
Houston, TX

We would also like to thank Officer John Radabaugh of the Delaware, Ohio, Police Department for his help in the preparation of this book.

Some words are shown in bold, **like this.**
You can find them in the picture glossary on page 23.

Contents

What Do Police Officers Do?

Police officers help keep people safe.

They help you cross the street safely.

Police officers help when something goes wrong.

This police officer is helping at an **accident**.

What Is a Police Officer's Day Like?

Police officers go on patrol.

They watch out for trouble.

Police officers help people who
are lost.

They write reports at the
police station.

What Do Police Officers Wear?

name tag

badge

Police officers wear **uniforms.**

Badges and **name tags** tell people who they are.

Police officers often wear white gloves while **directing traffic.**

White gloves help drivers see the officer.

What Tools Do Police Officers Use?

Police officers use a **two-way radio** to talk to each other.

They use **computers** in their **squad cars.**

This police officer is using a **laser**.

It shows how fast a car is moving.

Where Do Police Officers Work?

Police officers work at police stations.

Some towns have only one small police station.

Large cities have many police stations.

These stations are very busy.

Do Police Officers Work in Other Places?

Sometimes police officers work in schools.

They teach children about safety.

They work at airports and
train stations.

These police officers work at
the beach.

When Do Police Officers Work?

There are always police officers working.

Some work during the day, and others work at night.

Police officers rush to help.

They must always be ready.

What Kinds of Police Officers Are There?

Beat cops walk along the streets.

Patrol officers often drive squad cars.

Mounted police ride horses.

Some police officers ride bicycles.

How Do People Become Police Officers?

People go to special schools to become police officers.

They go to class and study.

They exercise to keep in shape.

Police officers are people who like
to help others.

Quiz

Can you remember what these things are called?

Look for the answers on page 24.

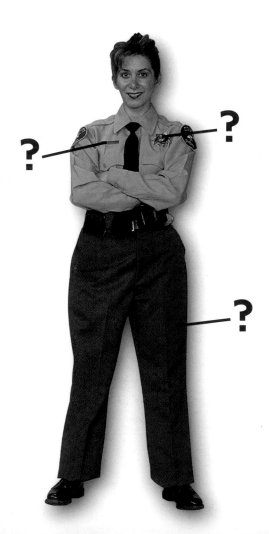

? ? ?

Picture Glossary

accident
page 5

directing traffic
page 9

patrol officer
page 18

badge
page 8

laser
page 11

squad car
(skwad kar)
pages 10, 18

beat cop
page 18

mounted police
page 19

two-way radio
page 10

computer
page 10

name tag
page 8

uniform
page 8

Note to Parents and Teachers

Reading for information is an important part of a child's literacy development. Learning begins with a question about something. Help children think of themselves as investigators and researchers by encouraging their questions about the world around them. Each chapter in this book begins with a question. Read the question together. Look at the pictures. Talk about what you think the answer might be. Then read the text to find out if your predictions were correct. Think of other questions you could ask about the topic, and discuss where you might find the answers. Assist children in using the picture glossary and the index to practice new vocabulary and research skills.

Index

Answers to quiz on page 22

name tag

badge

uniform